NAM

The Vietnam War

The Johnson Years
1965–1968

Published by Brown Bear Books Ltd

4877 N. Circulo Bujia
Tucson, AZ 85718
USA

and

First Floor
9-17 St. Albans Place
London N1 0NX

ISBN: 978-1-78121-043-7

Library of Congress Cataloging-in-Publication Data
available upon request

Editorial Director: Lindsey Lowe
Managing Editor: Tim Cooke
Design Manager: Keith Davis
Designer: Lynne Lennon
Picture Manager: Sophie Mortimer
Children's Publisher: Anne O'Daly
Production Director: Alastair Gourlay

Manufactured in the United States of America

CPSIA compliance information: Batch# AG/5506

Contents

INTRODUCTION

The first major group of U.S. ground forces arrived in Vietnam in March 1965. Almost at once, things began to go wrong. President Lyndon B. Johnson knew a ground war would be unpopular with U.S. public opinion, but his advisors argued that it would be short and sharp. It was soon clear that they were mistaken.

Global contest

The Americans had become involved in the conflict between North and South Vietnam because of the Cold War. This was a contest for global influence between the United States and its allies on one hand and the Soviet Union and its allies on the other.

In 1954, North Vietnam had been created as a Communist state led by Ho Chi Minh, and supported by China and the Soviet Union. U.S. policy makers worried about the so-called domino theory. This broadly argued that, if one country in a region became Communist, there was an increased chance that its neighbors would follow suit.

Growing U.S. involvement

The first U.S. involvement had been to send special forces to support the South Vietnamese Army (Army of the Republic of Vietnam, or ARVN). The ARVN was fighting

▶ U.S. infantry climb down a ladder to clear a helicopter landing zone in January 1967.

▲ U.S. troops are evacuated after a mission against the Viet Cong in March 1966.

the Northern Vietnamese Army (NVA) and its allies, the Viet Cong (VC). The VC were Communists within South Vietnam who fought a guerrilla war against the South Vietnamese government.

Now U.S. ground troops faced the same enemy. But the NVA and VC fought an unconventional kind of warfare. There were few battles for territory. They melted away in the face of the enemy, only to reappear later. The Communists planned to fight a long war. They believed dissatisfaction at home would eventually undermine the U.S. war effort.

An unpopular conflict

That was what happened. As more U.S. troops poured into Vietnam and casualties rose, the unpopularity of the war rose at home. Johnson had been right to be concerned about public opinion. Vietnam came to dominate his presidency. The war's unpopularity was one of the reasons for his decision not to contest the 1968 presidential election, which was won by the Republican candidate, Richard M. Nixon. Nixon would inherit the ongoing conflict in Vietnam.

Chapter 1

The First U.S. Actions

The first American ground troops in Vietnam soon discovered that they faced an elusive enemy.

The arrival of the first U.S. combat troops in Vietnam in March 1965 confirmed President Lyndon B. Johnson's commitment to war. Johnson had hesitated before he accepted that it wolud be necessary to send in ground forces. Still, his military advisors informed him that the Americans would be able to fight a quick, intense war. The Johnson administration therefore argued that the war would be a limited operation, with only a limited mobilization of resources and men. They hoped that it would have

▼ U.S. Marines board a helicopter at Da Nang in April 1965 to be airlifted to a nearby position.

little impact on U.S. daily life. But by the end of 1965, more than 148,300 U.S. combat troops had been deployed to South Vietnam, and the Vietnam War was becoming a central feature of life for millions of Americans.

In North Vietnam, meanwhile, Ho Chi Minh and his ruling Communist Party had a very different view. They followed the theory of revolutionary war developed by Mao Zedong, now the leader of neigboring China. Mao argued that the way to win a revolution was by a long, drawn-out war that began with guerrilla action and only later involved conventional battles. For Ho, the objectives of the war were clear: to overthrow the government of South Vietnam and reunite the country. But he saw that the United States had no such clearly defined objectives. He also believed, following Mao's

▲ Marine tanks shell Viet Cong positions near Da Nang. The enemy melted away in the face of such assaults, but soon returned.

philosophy, that a democratic power would find it difficult to support a long war. The longer fighting went on, and casualties rose, the more unpopular the war would be at home. Eventually the public would demand a negotiated settlement, when Ho would be granted concessions. The North Vietnamese therefore settled in for the long haul.

View from the North

On June 27, 1965, General Westmoreland, commander of U.S. forces in Southeast Asia, launched the first offensive operation by U.S. ground troops in Vietnam. He wanted

▲ U.S. Marines cross farmland on a search-and-destroy operation against the Viet Cong in June 1965.

to clear a region just northwest of Saigon where the Viet Cong (VC) were believed to be particularly influential. After a year or more of using special forces to try to win support for the U.S. cause in the villages of Vietnam, Westmoreland had decided that it was time to become more aggressive.

Such aggression was more closely in line with U.S. military doctrine in the mid–1960s. U.S. soldiers were trained to carry out offensive warfare. The military commanders in Vietnam were not equipped, mentally or physically, to stay on the defensive. This would inevitably cause problems, because

their stated role in Vietnam—of protecting South Vietnam from interference by North Vietnam or the Viet Cong guerrillas—was a defensive one.

Search and destroy

Westmoreland ordered the 173rd Airborne Brigade to make a combined invasion with South Vietnamese (ARVN) units of War Zone D (Vietnam had been divided into four zones for military planning). Two U.S. battalions were to carry out an air assault into Landing Zone North, 16 miles (25 km) north of Bien Hoa. They would move south on a four-day "search and destroy" mission. Meanwhile two South Vietnamese battalions were to seek out and destroy enemy bases from Helicopter Landing Zone (HLZ) South,

▶ A napalm strike against a Viet Cong position. Napalm was a chemical jelly that clung to and burned the skin.

about 3 miles (5 km) to the southwest. Australian troops were based at Bien Hoa, ready to deploy in an hour if required.

On June 28, 1965, following air and artillery bombardments, the U.S. and South Vietnamese units flew into their landing zones. For two days, they searched for the enemy. They found lots of evidence of VC activity—ammunition, weapons, and large quantities of food—but no VC. The mission seemed to be a success. The enemy had not been confident enough to launch an attack, and the U.S. and ARVN troops had worked together well. Next time, however, the enemy would stand and fight.

KEY THEMES

ARVN

The Army of the Republic of Vietnam (ARVN) was trained by the French and U.S. military. During the 1960s, the United States supplied it with large amounts of equipment. Despite being well trained and equipped, the ARVN was weakened by corruption. Privates often looted supplies to supplement their pay; officers ran operations for financial gain. A lack of leadership and inexperience meant they were no match for the Viet Cong. At its peak, the ARVN numbered more than a million troops: 450,000 in the regular army, regional forces (similar to the National Guard), and the Civilian Irregular Defense Groups.

▶ The U.S. built bases around South Vietnam to support military air operations. This is an airstrip for Hercules cargo aircraft at An Khe.

KEY PERSONALITY
Lyndon B. Johnson

Johnson became president of the United States in 1963, following the assassination of John F. Kennedy. Despite an election pledge in 1964 not to widen U.S. involvement in Vietnam, he oversaw a huge expansion in U.S. activity in the war. This made Johnson very unpopular. On March 31, 1968, he anounced that he was requesting peace talks, and would not be standing for re-election. He died of a heart attack just before the peace agreement was signed in January 1973.

Operation Starlite

The first major battle of the Vietnam War started on August 17, 1965. During July it had become evident that the Viet Cong were massing south of Chu Lai, a U.S. Marine base 56 miles (90 km) southeast of Da Nang. Operation Starlite was designed to destroy the 1st VC Regiment in the area and prevent any attack on the base. The U.S. 7th Marine Regiment launched a three-pronged attack by helicopter and amphibious assault. The Marines came under heavy mortar and rifle fire, which left five dead and 17 wounded. By the time enemy fire had been suppressed, the Marines attacked to find that the enemy had fled, although there were pockets of resistance from groups of VC soldiers hidden in bunkers and caves.

The United States had scored a resounding victory: almost 700 Viet Cong soldiers were killed. U.S. losses stood at 45 dead and more than 200 wounded. The battle had made it clear to both sides that the Viet Cong would not be able to defeat the Marines in a stand-up battle; the VC would need to change their strategy. The defeat had also forced them inland from their bases along the coastline.

Struggle in the highlands

From September 1965, three North Vietnamese Army (NVA) regiments operated in the Central Highlands of South Vietnam. Their mission was to split South Vietnam in two before the Americans built up their troop numbers. On the night of October 19, 1965, the NVA attacked the U.S. Special Forces Camp at Plei Mei, which was key to controlling the Central Highlands. After the attackers seized part of the camp, the U.S. 1st Air Cavalry Division (Airmobile) was deployed to the area and held on to the camp. The stage was set for the Battle of Ia Drang, the most significant engagement of 1965.

▼ **U.S. Marines advance cautiously during a search-and-destroy mission near the village of Pho Thuong, a rumored site of Viet Cong activity.**

Battle of Ia Drang

The Battle of Ia Drang (November 14–18) was one of the first major clashes between the U.S. Army and the North Vietnamese Army (NVA). It was the second significant mission of General Westmoreland's search-and-destroy policy. He wanted to secure Landing Zone X-Ray, which was vulnerable to enemy forces on the surrounding high ground.

Three U.S. Army battalions clashed with two NVA regiments. The Americans were supported by massive artillery bombardments and airstrikes by B-52 Stratofortress bombers based on Guam. Eventually, elements of the 66th North Vietnamese Regiment moved east toward Plei Mei, where they ambushed three U.S. infantry battalions on November 17. The Americans fought their way out in desperate hand-to-hand fighting. They suffered 60 percent casualties, losing one in every three soldiers dead. Despite such losses, the U.S. victory convinced Westmoreland that his search and destroy"policy was correct.

Meanwhile, the month-long Operation Silver Bayonet was launched in October 1965. The U.S. 1st Cavalry Division (Airmobile) aimed to destroy the NVA in the Central Highlands. By the time the operation ended in November, casualties for Operation Silver Bayonet stood at 1,771 enemy killed and wounded and 200 U.S. soldiers killed and wounded.

◄ A 105mm self-propelled howitzer of the 3rd Marine Division shells VC positions. U.S. artillery and air strikes took a heavy toll of the enemy in 1965.

◀ UH-1 Huey helicopters carry men of the U.S. 1st Cavalry Division into action against the NVA in October 1965.

Growing commitment

The United States had won the early military engagements. But the determination of the NVA and VC, and their willingness to suffer high casualties, made it clear to U.S. commanders in Vietnam that they could only ensure the South's survival with a massive increase in U.S. military aid.

Already, the original idea that the conflict would be short and limited seemed over optimistic. By December 1965, the number of U.S. troops in Vietnam had risen to almost 200,000, compared with just 3,500 in March of that year.

KEY PERSONALITY

William Westmoreland

A 1936 graduate of the U.S. Military Academy, Westmoreland was commander of the Strategic Army Corps and XVIII Airborne Corps from 1963 to 1964. He became commander of the U.S. Military Command Assistance at the peak of the Vietnam War, between 1964 and 1968. His strategy was to seek and destroy the enemy, while also bombing industrial and strategic targets in North Vietnam. He was chief of staff of the U.S. Army from July 3, 1968, to June 30, 1972, and supervised the eventual withdrawal of U.S. troops from Vietnam.

Battles of 1966-1967

The first hostilities between U.S. and Communist forces showed there would be no easy victory for either side.

The first two full years of the war—1966 and 1967—were a period of growing disillusionment for many Americans. Despite President Johnson's hopes for a short, limited conflict, it seemed that the United States was becoming bogged down in a war it did not seem to be winning. No matter how many U.S. troops were sent to Vietnam—and by the end of 1967 there were almost half a million American troops in Vietnam—the Viet Cong (VC) and the North Vietnamese Army (NVA) had a response.

The enemy could not match U.S. firepower or maneuverability in pitched battles. That did not stop them, however. They continued to fight small-scale actions or used guerrilla tactics. A seemingly endless flow of men and materials entered South Vietnam via the infamous Ho Chi Minh Trail. Every year 200,000 North Vietnamese men came of age and enlisted. Increasingly, too, General

▲ U.S. troops raced from a helicopter. Landing was often risky, because the enemy swept helicopter landing zones with gunfire.

▲ A. U.S. Skyraider drops a phosphorus bomb. Phosphorus burns fiercely, making it an effective antipersonnel weapon.

Westmoreland's "search and destroy" tactic was failing. The Communists started most of the fights: they chose the place and the time to their advantage. The Americans could only fight back on the defensive. Throughout 1966, President Johnson repeatedly offered to attend peace talks but the North Vietnamese insisted that the U.S. bombing must stop before they would attend, so the process constantly stalled.

Operation Crimp

On January 8, 1966, the Americans launched the largest operation of the war to date. The goal of Operation Crimp, which deployed almost 8,000 troops of the 173rd Airborne

▶ A U.S. soldier sights along his M60 machine gun. The M60 could fire up to 550 rounds per minute.

KEY THEMES

Fire support bases

There were no real frontlines in Vietnam so infantry operations were supported by a series of fire support bases. These heavily fortified temporary camps provided artillery support to infantry operating in areas beyond their normal range of fire support. The NVA and VC frequently attacked the bases. To protect them, the U.S. Army deployed 65 battalions of artillery.

Brigade and other elements of the 1st Division, was to capture the Viet Cong's headquarters in Saigon, reputed to be in the district of Chu Chi. Despite razing Chu Chi, the Americans failed to find the base. It was later discovered that the VC hid in an extensive network of underground tunnels. More frustrating for the U.S. commanders was the reminder that the Viet Cong could avoid full-scale battles if it chose to. At the same time, the largest search-and destroy-operation so far failed to inflict appreciable casualties on the enemy. It lasted 42 days and used a massive amount of firepower, but did not accomplish much apart from increasing the number of refugees fleeing the violence.

In March, attention focused to the A Shau valley, near the border with Laos. The U.S. forces maintained a CIDG camp there to carry out border surveillance. On March 9 and 10, the NVA attacked the camp, which the Americans abandoned after a two-day battle. It would be two years before the Allied forces retook the valley.

Setbacks on the ground were met by increased efforts in the air. On June 29, the

▶ A 105mm battery opens fire in February, 1966. Artillery provided invaluable support to infantry units in battle.

U.S. Air Force (USAF) bombed industrial targets around Hanoi and Haiphong in an expansion of Operation Rolling Thunder. A week later, the North Vietnamese paraded 52 U.S. prisoners of war through Hanoi. The U.S. public was outraged. Pressure increased on the Johnson administration as the war grew even more unpopular.

The NVA 324th Division now made an assault into the Demilitarized Zone (DMZ), but were repulsed by U.S. forces and their South Vietnamese allies. The whole U.S. 3rd Marine Division moved north and established a forward headquarters at Dong Hain in northern Quang Tri province. In November, the Marines established a one-battalion base near the U.S. Special Forces camp in northwest Quang Tri province. The bases's name would shortly become one of the most famous in the Marines' illustrious history: Khe Sanh (see page 30).

KEY THEMES

Ho Chi Minh Trail

The Ho Chi Minh Trail was an intricate system of paths used by North Vietnam to infiltrate troops and supplies into South Vietnam, Cambodia, and Laos during the Vietnam War. The majority of the route ran through Laos and crossed challenging mountainous and jungle terrain. The volume of traffic expanded greatly at the start of the 1960s, but it still took a month to march from North to South Vietnam. By 1974, stretches of the trail were paved and had underground support facilities such as hospitals and fuel storage tanks. In 1975, it was the major supply route for the successful North Vietnamese invasion of the South.

Escalating conflict

By the end of 1966, there were more than 400,000 American military personnel in Vietnam. There had been a tenfold increase in U.S. military activity but the enemy was not only growing but also better becoming equipped. The Soviets were supplying the NVA with AK-47 Kalashnikov assault rifles and RP-2s (rocket propelled grenade launchers). Soviet 120mm heavy mortars allowed the communists to launch attacks on major U.S. military installations throughout the South,

The escalation would continue through 1967. More Communist soldiers penetrated into South Vietnam, forcing U.S. forces to increase the pace of operations against them and the Viet Cong. U.S. and South Vietnamese forces continued offensives into the DMZ. Marines in I Corps Tactical

KEY THEMES

Search and Destroy

Search and destroy was a tactic developed by General William Westmoreland and his deputy, Brigadier-General William Depuy. The idea was that U.S. forces would use extremely heavy firepower to inflict losses on the North Vietnamese Army (NVA) and the Viet Cong (VC). Helicopters, backed by artillery and air power, would destroy enemy forces rather than trying to capture territory. It was an aggressive tactic in which U.S. units would "find, fix, and finish" their enemy. But it ultimately failed. The Communists, tended to choose the location and time of their attacks. They also had a vast supply of manpower to replace any losses.

◀ **U.S. Marines cross a stream as they advance in Quang Tri Province, northwest of Dong Ha.**

Zone started offensives to cut off NVA movement into the Northern and Central Highlands. In September 1967, U.S. Defense Secretary Robert McNamara announced the construction of the McNamara Line to block Communist infiltration of the eastern DMZ. It would be a series of electronic sensors and warning systems. Despite such measures, Hanoi kept sending men and supplies down the Ho Chi Minh Trail. In the South, the Viet Cong continued to wage a brutal war against Saigon and the U.S. troops.

Operation Cedar Falls

In January 1967, U.S. commanders launched Operation Cedar Falls. The 173rd, 1st Infantry, 25th Infantry, 11th Armored Cavalry, and ARVN forces took on the Viet Cong in the so-called Iron Triangle, a VC-controlled area between the Saigon River and Route 13. The operation, which lasted 19 days, was a success that demonstrated the potential value of longer operations within VC-controlled areas. Hundreds of enemy fortifications were destroyed and large quantities of supplies

▼ **A special forces detachment uses a flat-bottomed airboat to patrol in the Mekong Delta.**

► U.S. Airborne troops guard Viet Cong fighters captured during Operation Cedar Falls. More than 500 suspected fighteres were captured during the operation.

and food were captured. But most of the VC fighters themselves managed to escape by crossing through the Allied lines.

Fight at Khe Sanh

On April 24, 1967, a major battle broke out at Khe Sanh. Khe Sanh was strategically important: it was close to the North Vietnamese supply route to the South, the Ho Chi Minh Trail. Sitting on top of a plateau in the shadow of Dong Tri Mountain, it overlooked a tributary of the Quang Tri River, making it a valuable observation post.

May 3 saw some of the heaviest fighting of the Vietnam War to date. U.S. Marines succeeded in taking Hill 881N, northwest of the base, which gave them a good view

KEY PERSONALITY

Robert Macnamara

McNamara was president of the Ford Motor Company before he resigned in 1960 to join the Kennedy administration as secretary of defense. An initial supporter of U.S. involvement in Vietnam, by 1966 McNamara was questioning the wisdom of increasing military involvement. By 1967, he was actively seeking peace negotiations.

of the enemy's infiltration routes. The 3rd Marines got rid of all NVA forces in the area by May 11; they had fired more than 25,000 rounds of ammunition. But the NVA was not put off. They continued to mass around the base to prepare for another attack.

Another major engagement was fought at the firebase at Con Thien, "Hill of Angels," 2 miles (3.2 km) south of the DMZ. In September 1967, the NVA began a major assault. On September 25, 1,200 shells hit the base in one of the heaviest North Vietnamese artillery bombardments. The assault marked the first phase of the Communist campaign that would last through the winter and spring, culminating in the Tet Offensive of 1968. Although the Marines held the base, the constant bombardment wore down morale.

At the battle of Loc Ninh, which started on October 29, VC forces

attacked Loc Ninh, a South Vietnamese CIDG. U.S. firepower again saved an isolated outpost; 800 Viet Cong and 15 Americans were killed.

By the end of 1967 almost half a U.S. million troops were stationed in Vietnam. As the war expanded, so did the antiwar movement. In April 1967, more than 300,000 people demonstrated against the war in New York City. Across the United States support for the war was falling: by the fall, only 35 percent of Americans supported the war.

► This Huey Cobra gunship has been fitted with rocket pods that can fire salvoes of multiple rockets against ground targets.

Chapter 3

Rolling Thunder

The Americans hoped to bomb North Vietnam into submission. Despite causing huge damage, they failed.

Operation Rolling Thunder was part of a strategic bombing campaign in which United States military aircraft attacked targets throughout North Vietnam. It was originally planned to last only eight weeks. As things turned out, the U.S. 2nd Air Division (later the 7th Airforce), the U.S. Navy, and the Republic of Vietnam Air Force (VNAF) carried out heavy bombardments of North Vietnamese targets from March 2, 1965, until November 2, 1968.

Rolling Thunder began before the U.S. administration of President Lyndon B. Johnson committed ground troops to the conflict. It initially had four main objectives. These were to boost the morale of America's

▼ An A-1E Skyraider drops a napalm bomb on a Viet Cong position that has already been hit by U.S. bombs.

KEY MOMENT

B-52 Stratofortress

The Boeing B-52F was a high-altitude radar bomber. Its first action was on June 18, 1965, when 27 B-52Fs from Andersen AFB, Guam, hit Viet Cong strongholds at Ben Cat, north of Saigon, during Operation Arc Light. By the end of the year, Arc Light had flown more than 1,500 sorties in South Vietnam. It then bombed Laos in December 1965 and North Vietnam from April 1966. Military opinion was divided over the effectiveness of using B-52s for tactical purposes.

◀ Helicopters airlift infantry into action. Vietnam was the first war in which helicopters played an essential role.

Minh Trail. The Johnson administration expected the Communists of North Vietnam to capitulate immediately. One senior U.S. general, Curtis LeMay, later argued that the United States should bomb Vietnam "back to the Stone Age." But despite the most intense air battle fought by U.S. troops since World War II, the predicted result failed to occur.

Johnson gives in

Following his re-election in November 1964, Johnson had resisted calls to retaliate against raids and attacks carried out by the Communists. However, when the Viet Cong attacked U.S. installations at Pleiku on February 7, 1965, the president finally authorized more air strikes against North

allies in the Saigon government in South Vietnam; to persuade the North Vietnamese to stop their support for the insurgents in South Vietnam without committing U.S. ground troops for an invasion of North Vietnam; to destroy North Vietnam's fledgling industrial base, its transportation system, and air defenses; and to stop men and supplies getting into South Vietnam via the Ho Chi

◀ B-52 Stratofortresses rain bombs on their targets. Each B-52 could carry up to 70,000 pounds (31,500 kg) of bombs.

Vietnamese targets. On March 2, 1965, Operation Rolling Thunder began officially, but there had already been an air strike on February 24, 1965, when 100 U.S. aircraft attacked targets in North Vietnam. Early U.S. air strikes also hit the Ho Chi Minh Trail, the Communist supply line which ran mainly through the neighboring country of Laos.

Restricted campaign

The Johnson administration imposed strict limits on the targets that could be hit, however. Johnson's advisers were concerned that, if China and the Soviet Union thought North Vietnam faced defeat, they might intervene. As a result, the administration tried to punish the North without provoking the

two nations it believed were North Vietnam's protectors and suppliers.

From the start, Washington decided which targets could be hit. Washington determined the day and hour of the attack, which aircraft would be used, which ordnance, and in which quantities. It also decreed that there was a 30-nautical-mile (37.5 mile/60 km) exclusion zone around Hanoi and a 10-nautical-mile (12 mile/19 km) exclusion zone around the port of Haiphong. Washington also stipulated a a 30-mile (48-km) buffer zone along the length of the Chinese border.

Although some of these restrictions would later be lifted, Johnson continued to keep tight control over the whole operation, much to the irritation of his chiefs of staff.

They thought that one of the most important military strategies was the destruction of the port of Haiphong. Johnson refused to authorize its bombing, however, and it was not until 1972 that such an operation was implemented.

The campaign begins

The first mission on March 2, 1965, was against an ammunition storage area near Xom Bang. The same day, 19 VNAF A-1 Skyraiders hit the Quang Khe Naval Base. The Americans were stunned when six aircraft were shot down during the mission.

▼ Ground crew at Bien Hoa Air Base fill aerial tanks with napalm for use against the enemy in May 1966.

KEY THEMES

Helicopters

Helicopters were first used in Vietnam in January 1962. Their role became increasingly important as the war continued. The workhorse of the war, the UH-1 Huey, was used to transport troops and supplies and to evacuate the wounded. In 1968, the AH-1 Cobra arrived. It was a purpose-built helicopter gunship. Vietnam was the first helicopter war: the combined forces of the U.S. Military flew over 30 million sorties.

KEY THEMES

Agent Orange

One of the weapons the Americans used in the air war was Agent Orange, a herbicide. The chemical killed trees and bushes to prevent the enemy being able to hide in them. As well as devastating the countryside, however, Agent Orange also contained chemicals that were poisonous to humans. Many Americans who handled the bombs and Vietnamese victims of the bombing later developed cancers caused by Agent Orange.

The majority of U.S. air strikes were launched from four air bases in Thailand: Korat, Takhli, Udon Thani, and Ubon. Aircraft refueled from aerial tankers over Laos before flying to North Vietnam. They bombed their targets before either turning around and flying straight back to Thailand or flying on over the Gulf of Tonkin. Naval airstrikes were carried out at much shorter ranges: aircraft took off from the carriers of Task Force 77 off the North Vietnamese coast.

On April 3, the Joint Chiefs persuaded Defense Secretary Robert McNamara and President Johnson to launch a four-

▼ Phosphorous bombs explode among Viet Cong positions in May 1966.

◀ A B-52 Stratofortress drops its bombs from high altitude.

week attack on North Vietnamese lines of communications. Their aim was to isolate North Vietnam from overland supplies sent from China and the Soviet Union. The raids destroyed 26 bridges and seven ferries. Attacks on southern North Vietnam increased dramatically, with the number of sorties rising from 2 to 200 per week by the end of 1965.

Despite all of this, after the first few weeks of heavy bombardment it was apparent that Operation Rolling Thunder so far had failed to weaken the enemy's will to fight. On April 8, North Vietnam's Premier Pham Van Dong refused to enter peace negotiations while the bombing continued.

A secondary role

When U.S. ground troops arrived at Da Nang on March 8, 1965, Operation Rolling Thunder became a secondary part of the war. From now on, the aerial attacks were always subordinate to ground attacks and targets could be changed at any moment. By December 1965, 170 U.S. aircraft and 8

VNAF aircraft had been lost; 25,971 sorties had been flown, and 32,063 tons of bombs had been dropped.

On June 29, 1966, Johnson authorized air strikes against petroleum, oil, and lubricant (POL) storage areas in North Vietnam. His military chiefs had long been asking for the strikes. At first they appeared successful, but by September it was clear that the North Vietnamese were not suffering from fuel shortages and so the air strikes were stopped. By the spring of 1967, McNamara and others in the administration were convinced that Operation Rolling Thunder in general was not working.

Expanding the mission

McNamara and his allies opposed the generals who wanted to intensify the bombing and loosen the target restrictions. For their part, the generals claimed the bombing was working. At the same time, they demanded greater freedom in their choice of targets. On July 20, 1967, a revised Rolling Thunder target list was issued. It allowed air attacks on 16 additional fixed targets and 23 road, rail, and waterway links inside the restricted Hanoi–Haiphong area. Between August 13 and 19, 1967, B-52 bombers dropped bombs on strategic targets such as bridges, bypasses, rail yards, and military storage areas in an effort to stop traffic between Hanoi and Haiphong. The bombing destroyed around 30 percent of the North's railroad system.

▶ B-52s carry out a raid. The bombers attacked both strategic targets and enemy ground positions.

Opposition at home

In the United States disquiet about Operation Rolling Thunder continued to grow. On August 9, 1967, the Senate Armed Services Committee opened hearings on the bombing campaign. The military chiefs complained that the build-up of the air war had been too gradual and that it had been handicapped by the civilian-imposed restrictions. McNamara told the committee that there was no evidence

▶ This bridge in North Vietnam was destroyed by U.S. bombing in Operation Rolling Thunder.

F-105 Thunderchief

Nicknamed the "Thud," the Thunderchief flew more than 20,000 combat missions in Vietnam. More than 350 aircraft were lost in combat, most to North Vietnamese antiaircraft artillery. It could carry eight 750lb bombs on long-range missions and 16 on short-range missions. An F-105 pilot stood only a 75 percent chance of surviving 100 missions over North Vietnam.

that the bombing campaign would ultimately succeed in forcing the North Vietnamese regime into submission.

No longer supporting U.S. policy in the war, McNamara resigned as secretary of defense in February 1968. Within two months, however, his successor, Clark Clifford, began to agree with his predecessor. Clifford could not see how this open-ended commitment to war in Vietnam could succeed. Johnson, facing an election and aware that political defeat loomed for his

Democratic Party, was eager to get Hanoi to the negotiating table. He announced on March 31, 1968, that all bombing north of the 19th Parallel would stop.

End of the operation

U.S. bombers now turned their attention to bombing between the 17th and 19th Parallels. Pilots flew more than 6,000 sorties per month. Meanwhile, the North Vietnamese finally agreed to meet the Americans for peace talks in Paris. President Johnson immediately declared that all bombing of North Vietnam would stop on November 1, 1968. Rolling Thunder was over.

Chapter 4

The Siege of Khe Sanh

A remote base near the DMZ would become the site of a battle the Americans hoped would prove decisive in the war.

The Khe Sanh combat base was one of the most remote bases of all U.S. bases in Vietnam, and it became the location of one of the most famous military actions of the war.

Khe Sanh was located in Quang Tri Province in a mountainous region at the extreme northwest corner of Vietnam, near to both the Demilitarized Zone (DMZ) and the border with Laos. It was of great strategic importance because it lay at the start of the Ho Chi Minh Trail into South Vietnam. The trail was the main route used by the Communists to infiltrate troops and supplies from the North to fighters in South. Green Beret Special Forces had established a base there in August 1962 on top of a plateau

▲ This view was taken from a helicopter flying over the position of the 1st Battalion, 9th Marine Regiment, at Khe Sanh.

in the shadow of Dong Tri Mountain. Its location made it a good observation post from which road-watch teams monitored North Vietnamese Army (NVA) activity in Laos. The base was also a platform from which to launch special operations missions.

In spring 1967 the Khe Sanh airstrip was improved to handle larger airplanes. The base

◄ Smoke and dust envelop the base at Khe Sanh during a North Vietnamese rocket attack n February.

had its own artillery support. It also lay within range of the 175-mm guns of Camp Carroll, which was located to the east.

General William Westmoreland, commander of U.S. military operations, saw Khe Sanh not only as part of the defensive perimeter, preventing NVA and communist infiltration. He also saw as a good location from which to hit the enemy with close air support, artillery fire, and machine-gun fire.

The first battle

On April 24, 1967, a fierce battle broke out when Communists attacked Khe Sanh. The 3rd Marines arrived to reinforce the base, and an additional artillery battery was also sent. The Marines set out to establish a perimeter on the hills surrounding the base, sparking some of the heaviest fighting of the war. But the Marines captured a hill northwest of the base form which they could clearly observe

KEY THEMES

Montagnards

Montagnard is a French word meaning "highlander" or "mountain man". It refers to any member of the hill-dwelling peoples of Indochina. Their unique culture is centered village life, and they practise slash-and-burn agriculture. They believe in nature and ancestors spirits, which they contact with shamans and sorcerers. In Vietnam, the Montagnards are one of the largest minority groups, with more than 100 tribes. The Montagnards are very hostile toward the lowland Vietnamese, and want to be independent from them. During the Vietnam War they sided with the Americans and South Vietnamese.

the enemy's infiltration routes. The Marines had cleared the hills of all NVA forces by May 11. U.S. firepower proved decisive: the 1st Marine Aircraft Wing flew more than 1,110 sorties and dropped 1,900 tons (1,930 t) of bombs on a series of concrete-reinforced NVA fortifications around the base. While Marine aircraft provided close air support, the U.S. Air Force carried out 23 B-52 strikes against enemy troop concentrations, supply lines, and ammunition depots. Despite this heavy bombardment, the NVA was not put off. It spent the rest of 1967 regrouping and rearming for another attack.

Strategic decision

In Washington, D.C., President Johnson was taking a personal interest in the base at Khe Sanh. It had become apparent that the NVA was preparing for a full-scale siege. Initially, the U.S. command in Saigon thought that the Battle of Khe Sanh had been an

▼ Keeping watch for Viet Cong booby traps, U.S. infantry cross a stream.

► A bomb dropped by a U.S. Air Force F-4 Phantom explodes near enemy positions just outside the perimeter at Khe Sanh.

isolated incident, but as the fall progressed it had become clear that the NVA was re-arming. The question was whether the U.S. should defend the base or abandon it to the Communists. The President and his military chiefs decided that the base should be held at all costs.

Preparing for action

By fall 1967, U.S. strength at Khe Sanh stood at one Marine infantry battalion reinforced with Marine and Army artillery and tanks. During December 1967 and January 1968, three more Marine battalions together with an ARVN Ranger battalion were airlifted to Khe Sanh. By late January, the base and surrounding fortified hill positions held 6,053 troops. On the morning of January 21, 1968, the NVA finally launched their long-anticipated assault. The siege of Khe Sanh had begun. It would last 77 days.

The assault began with a 100-round mortar and rocket attack on the base on January 21. The Marines' defenses were not fully prepared, and engineers hurriedly began to build trenches and to lay additional rows of concertina wire around the base's perimeter. At around 5.15 a.m., one or more Communist shells scored a direct hit on the base's ammunition dump. It set off an explosion of 16,000 artillery shells that made the national evening news across the United States.

Decisive battle

Westmoreland believed that Khe Sanh was the perfect place in Vietnam for a decisive battle: it was uninhabited by civilians, it was

▲ As enemy artillery explodes in the background, a U.S. Air Force C-130 Hercules delivers supplies to Khe Sanh.

KEY THEMES

The Barrier System and the DMZ

The Barrier System was proposed by Secretary of Defense Robert S. McNamara. Running alongside the Demilitarized Zone (DMZ), it was a 25-mile (40-km) barrier with infrared intrusion detectors and ground sensors. It was intended to help U.S. Marines to detect enemy incursions and movements at greater ranges. Work began on the anti-infiltration system in April 1967 and continued off-and-on until mid-1968. The devices provided targeting data for air and artillery strikes, as well as providing U.S. intelligence with timely information about possible enemy targets during the siege at Khe Sanh and the Tet Offensive.

remote, and there were no South Vietnamese facilities to be threatened. He intended to use the Marines as bait to lure the North Vietnamese to attack the base. Marine commanders were furious at the policy. They argued that the isolated base was too difficult to support. The disagreement caused a bitter rift between the U.S. Army and the Marines.

Meanwhile, General Vo Nguyen Giap, the North Vietnamese Minister of Defense and Commander of the Vietnam People's Army (VPA), believed that in order to succeed against the Americans, the North Vietnamese should use the same guerrilla tactics that had been so effective against the French in the First Indochina War. Historians still argue about whether Giap's aim at Khe Sanh was to overrun the base or simply to divert thousands of U.S. troops away from the heavily populated coastal areas. If his aim was the latter, it was successful.

Those who believe that Giap wanted to capture the base point to the heavy bombardments and the numbers of troops he committed. On the night of February 29–March 1, the NVA staged their largest massed attack on the Khe Sanh perimeter. This regiment-sized strike was broken up only after the Marines called in air

◀ U.S. Marines shelter in a trench as they wait to be airlifted from Khe Sanh in February.

► A U.S. Marine at Khe Sanh watches F-4 Phantoms making an airstrike against NVA units outside the base.

strikes and the attackers suffered massive casualties at the hands of overwhelming U.S. aerial firepower.

Over the course of the siege, U.S. aircraft dropped 5,000 bombs daily. The base could only be resupplied by air, and fog often hampered helicopter drops, making resupply more difficult. Even water had to be airlifted in to the besieged garrison. On one occasion, a helicopter crew panicked as it attempted to deliver water to Hill 861 (named for the hill's height in meters) and dropped the load. The thirsty soldiers had to look on as the water containers exploded mid-air.

End of the siege

By March 1968, U.S. commanders believed that the North Vietnamese were giving

up on Khe Sanh. Westmoreland told President Johnson on March 9 that enemy casualties were between 6,000 and 8,000. Westmoreland took this as proof that the embattled Marines were winning. His primary goal at Khe Sanh was to kill the NVA at a faster rate than they could be replaced. The official enemy death toll was 1,602, but U.S. intelligence placed the total at between 10,000 and 15,000.

In early April, Operation Pegasus began. It was intended to relieve the garrison at Khe Sanh. The 1st Cavalry (Airmobile) Division and a South Vietnamese battalion approached overland from the east and the south, while the Marines pushed westward to reopen Route 9. The siege finally ended on April 9, 1968, when U.S. forces met up. Two months later, as U.S. strategy changed, commanders decided to abandon the base that the Marines had fought so hard to keep in favor of a more easily defended position. Marine positions were bulldozed, the airstrip removed, and the bunkers were destroyed.

Official figures put U.S. casualties at 205 dead, 1,668 wounded, and 1 missing. Unofficial figures suggest that 1,000 dead and 4,500 wounded were more realistic statistics. The amount of ordnance used was staggering. On February 23 alone, NVA artillery fired more than 1,300 shells. In total, the U.S. artillery battalion at the base fired 158,891 rounds and B-52 bombers dropped 59,542 tons of munitions.

Both sides claimed victory at Khe Sanh. For the North Vietnamese, the siege was part of the winter–spring campaign that culminated in the Tet Offensive. For the Americans, it was a chance to kill the enemy faster than they could be replaced. For the Marines, it was a siege in which Marine folklore suggests that it was they who were the true aggressors, not the "besiegers" outside the perimeter.

▼ The Marines used flamethrowers and small arms to repel enemy units who got too close to the perimeter at Khe Sanh.

Chapter 5

The Tet Offensive

The biggest military operation of the whole war was launched by the Communists in January 1968.

The year 1968 marked the turning point of the Vietnam War. In September 1967, the Communists had attacked a number of U.S. garrisons in South Vietnam. General William Westmoreland, commander of the U.S. military in Southeast Asia, was delighted. He took the attacks as evidence that the North Vietnamese were now fighting in the open. That would allow his forces to come to grips with their elusive enemy.

The Communists had suffered heavy casualties in the attacks: around 90,000 men. Westmoreland assured President Lyndon B. Johnson that such losses were too big to be replaced immediately. But Westmoreland was wrong. The Communists had planned the attacks to divert U.S. troops from the towns

▶ U.S. Marines shelter behind a partially demolished wall during the Battle of Hue.

and cities of South Vietnam while the Viet Cong (VC) began massing a force of nearly 84,000 fighters near these urban centers.

Holiday attack

By January 1968, the attackers were assembled. The VC and North Vietnamese Army (NVA) were now ready to attack the militarily inferior forces of the South Vietnamese Army (ARVN), who defended the cities. The attack was timed to coincide with the Tet holiday.

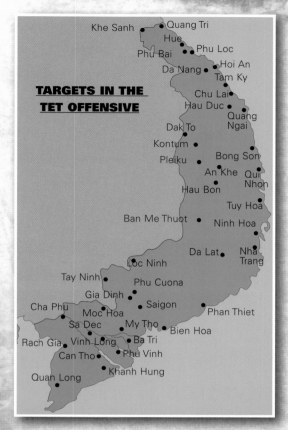

TARGETS IN THE TET OFFENSIVE

Khe Sanh • • Quang Tri
Hue •
Phu Bai • • Phu Loc
Da Nang • • Hoi An
• Tam Ky
Chu Lai •
Hau Duc •
• Quang Ngai
Dak To •
Kontum •
Pleiku • • Bong Son
An Khe • Qui Nhon
Hau Bon •
• Tuy Hoa
Ban Me Thuot • • Ninh Hoa
Da Lat • • Nha Trang
Loc Ninh •
Tay Ninh • Phu Cuona •
Gia Dinh •
Cha Phu • • Saigon
Moc Hoa • • Phan Thiet
Sa Dec • My Tho • • Bien Hoa
Rach Gia • Vinh Long • • Ba Tri
Can Tho • • Phu Vinh
Quan Long • • Khanh Hung

▲ The Tet Offensive saw coordinated Viet Cong attacks on every major town in South Vietnam.

Tet is an annual holiday when all Vietnamese pay tribute to their dead to mark the Lunar New Year. So far during the war, both sides had marked the holiday with a temporary ceasefire. In 1968, again, radio stations in North and South Vietnam announced a three-day ceasefire in honor of the Tet holiday. On January 21, 1968, the North Vietnamese attacked the U.S. combat base at Khe Sanh, but it was a diversion.

◄ The old Imperial City of Hue was devastated in the U.S. Marine operation to recapture the city from the Viet Cong.

KEY THEMES

Riverine Warfare

South Vietnam has many rivers, as well as the vast delta of the Mekong. The Viet Cong used the rivers to move around, and the U.S. Army and Navy resurrected the idea of river-based warfare, first used in the Civil War (1861–1865). Infantry units traveled by water and lived on ships, which were used as floating base camps. The Mobile Riverine Force or Task Force 117 was specially trained. This "brown-water navy" patrolled the waterways, hampering enemy movement.

Unknown to the Americans, the North Vietnamese had celebrated Tet early. The Viet Cong used the holiday ceasefire to infiltrate all the major cities of the South. On the morning of January 30, NVA and VC forces attacked some 100 towns and cities in South Vietnam, catching the South Vietnamese and Americans completely off guard. It became immediately apparent that the garrison attacks of the previous September had been carried out deliberately to clear urban areas of U.S. soldiers.

Gains in Saigon

The Tet Offensive was the largest military operation conducted by either side up to that point in the war. The initial attacks stunned the Allied forces and took them completely by surprise. The major target was the national capital, Saigon (now Ho Chi Minh City). Thirty-five battalions under General Tran Van Ta attacked the capital, focusing on targets of political and military importance. The attacks hoped to paralyze government control of the city and cause a general uprising. A 19-

man VC squad attacked the U.S. Embassy. Although they failed to get into the building, the attack stunned the U.S. public at home as they watched the fighting on live TV. Although embassy guards eventually killed the attackers following a six-hour battle, the Viet Cong had won a massive propaganda victory. The embassy was the symbol of U.S. power in Vietnam and the attack was broadcast across the world. It was clear that talk of an imminent U.S. victory in Vietnam was misguided, if not deliberate misinformation. The U.S. public increasingly wanted to withdraw from Vietnam, and antiwar protests would grow.

Across Saigon the Viet Cong made initial gains but a quick reaction by U.S. and ARVN forces meant that the gains were temporary. Fighting was particularly heavy at the strategically important Tan Son Nhut airbase, where there were high casualties.

Continued fighting

After the initial surprise, the Americans eventually managed to push back the Viet Cong throughout South Vietnam. There were exceptions where the fighting continued, however. The siege at the camp of Khe Sanh saw the defenders of the Marine Corps under attack for 77 days. Although the Communists

attacking the base suffered huge losses, their morale lasted far longer than the duration of the Tet Offensive. Similarly, the fight for the ancient capital city of Hue, in the center of the country, went on for 26 days.

▶ **A U.S. infantryman waits for action; he carries an antitank rocket launcher.**

Virtually everywhere else, the offensive was short lived. The local South Vietnamese failed to rise up in support of the Communists. Within 10 days, the Tet Offensive was over. Of the 84,000 Communist troops who had taken part, almost 58,000 had been killed. More specifically, the Viet Cong had almost been wiped out as a fighting force.

This would lead to the war taking a different direction. The remaining Viet Cong were forced to retreat to the highlands to regroup; they abandoned territory in the lowlands that they had controlled for years. From now on, the war would be controlled directly from Hanoi using the North Vietnamese Army (NVA).

▼ U.S. infantry and M113 armored personnel carriers engage the enemy in a firefight at Long Binh during the Tet Offensive.

KEY THEMES

Battle for Hue

The bloodiest action of the Tet Offensive came in Hue, the cultural center of Vietnam. The headquarters of the ARVN 1st Division was located in the city, together with 200 U.S. troops and a few Australians. Fighting started on January 31, when NVA units attacked the Citadel and soon captured the Imperial Palace of Peace. Troops from the U.S. 1st Division were sent to relieve the city, backed by the U.S. 1st Cavalry Division. They met fierce Communist resistance. Two weeks of bitter street-fighting followed before the palace was finally recaptured on February 25.

▲ During the Tet Offensive, ARVN troops search for VC fighters in Nguyen Binh Khien Street in Saigon.

Positives for the South

For the South, the Tet Offensive had some positives. Both the ARVN and the U.S. Army had scored a significant tactical victory. The ARVN in particular had surprised the Communists by fighting well during the offensive. It had shown that it was now an effective fighting force, and not just an add-on to the U.S. Army.

General Westmoreland and President Johnson both felt that Tet marked a turning point in the war and that they were on the way to victory. Westmoreland now asked for more troops to be sent to ensure a final victory in Vietnam. Johnson was not expecting such a request. His Secretary of Defense, Robert McNamara, who was seen by many as the architect of U.S. policy in Vietnam, had already announced he was leaving the administration and that he had come to the conclusion that the war was a mistake. McNamara advised Johnson to reject Westmoreland's request. For his part, the president could not decide what to do. He would be required to call upon the National

43

◀ Residents in Saigon search through the rubble of their homes after a 122mm rocket attack.

▼ Young NVA prisoners captured during Tet attend a class in the Bien Hoa prison camp.

Guard to meet the troop numbers. This, he felt, would threaten the economic prosperity of the United States. Also, Johnson was aware that the U.S. public did not see the Tet Offensive as a great victory. The public had not seen any territory taken or victories won. What they had seen was the U.S. Embassy come under attack and many Americans die.

It was more proof to many Americans that their government had lied to them about the nature of the war. They took to the streets to protest.

Aftermath of Tet

Johnson asked his new Secretary of Defense, Clark Clifford, for his opinion. Clifford advised the president that not only should he refuse Westmoreland's request for troops but that he should consider the United States leaving Vietnam all together. On March 31, 1968, President Johnson adressed the U.S. people on live television. He stunned the watching audience when he announced that he was stopping Operation Rolling Thunder (the heavy bombing campaign against targets in North Vietnam) and would begin the gradual

KEY MOMENT

My Lai Massacre

The village of My Lai lay in an area of heavy Viet Cong activity. On March 16, 1968, the soldiers of C Company, 11th Brigade, American Division entered the village. Their "search and destroy" mission quickly turned into a brutal massacre of more than 300 unarmed civilians that included women, children, and the elderly. In September 1969, Lieutenant William Calley, who led the massacre, was charged with murder. Soon afterward, word of the massacre got out in the press. The U.S. public reacted to the news by asking more questions about the behavior of American soldiers in Vietnam and about the whole reason fro U.S. involvement in the war.

withdrawal of U.S. troops from Vietnam.

The aftermath of the Tet Offensive changed the course of the war. What the military leaders saw as a victory was seen as a failure back in the United States. Johnson's presidency was effectively over.

GLOSSARY

amphibious Describes a military operation in which troops are landed from the sea.

antipersonnel Weapons that are designed to kill and injure soldiers rather than damage hardware or fortifications.

artillery Large-bore weapons, such as cannons and howitzers.

bunkers Heavily fortified strongpoints that are either buried or partly buried in the ground.

delta A large triangular-shaped area formed at the mouth of a river and often cut by many water channels.

deploy To distribute military forces ready for action.

DMZ Abbreviation for "demilitarized zone," an area between North and South Vietnam before the outbreak of war in which neither side was supposed to station any troops.

garrison A body of troops positioned to guard a city or strongpoint.

guerrilla Someone who fights by irregular means such as ambush, sabotage, and assassination.

gunship A heavily armed airplane or helicopter that uses guns, rockets, and bombs to attack targets on the ground.

infiltration When an enemy passes unnoticed through a military line or position.

mobilization The preparation of an army to fight at the start of a conflict.

Montagnards Members of various hill peoples from central and southern Vietnam.

morale The fighting spirit of an individual or a group, and how much they believe in victory.

propaganda Information that is biased in order to persuade people to support or reject a particular cause.

"search and destroy" A U.S. military tactic in which patrols attempted to locate VC units in the countryside and then defeat them in a firefight.

strategic Something that is related to the overall course of a conflict, rather than to a short-term victory in a single battle.

Viet Cong A guerrilla member of the Vietnamese Communist movement.

FURTHER RESOURCES

Books

Gitlin, Marty. *U.S. Involvement in Vietnam* (Essential Events). Abdo Publishing Company, 2010.

Gunderson, Megan M. *Lyndon B. Johnson: 36th President of the United States* (United States Presidents). Abdo Publishing Company, 2009.

Kent, Deborah. *The Vietnam War: From Da Nang to Saigon* (The United States at War). Enslow Publishing Inc, 2011.

McNeese, Tim. *The Cold War and Postwar America, 1946–1963*. Chelsea House Publications, 2010.

O'Connell, Kim A. *Primary Source Accounts of the Vietnam War* (America's Wars through Primary Sources). Myreportlinks.com, 2006.

Tougas, Shelley. *Weapons, Gear, and Uniforms of the Vietnam War* (Edge Books). Capstone Press, 2012.

The Vietnam War (Perspectives on Modern World History). Greenhaven Press, 2011.

White, Ellen Emerson. *Into No-Man's Land; The Journal of Patrick Seamus Flaherty, United States Marine Corps, Khe Sanh, Vietnam, 1968*. Turtleback, 2012.

Wiest, Andrew. *The Vietnam War* (Essential Histories: War and Conflict in Modern Times). Rosen Publishing Group, 2008.

Websites

http://www.pbs.org/wgbh/amex/vietnam/
Online companion to the PBS series *Vietnam: A Television History*.

www.history.com/topics/vietnam-war
History.com page of links about the Vietnam War.

http://www.spartacus.schoolnet.co.uk/vietnam.htm
Spartacus Educational page with links to biographies and other articles.

INDEX